T004548

THE BEST OF
The Beatles

ISBN 978-0-7935-2146-3

HAL•LEONARD® CORPORATION

7777 W. BLUEMOUND RD. P.O. BOX 13819 MILWAUKEE, WI 53213

Visit Hal Leonard Online at
www.halleonard.com

CONTENTS

All My Loving

TROMBONE

Words and Music by JOHN LENNON
and PAUL McCARTNEY

ACROSS THE UNIVERSE

TROMBONE

Words and Music by JOHN LENNON
and PAUL McCARTNEY

ALL YOU NEED IS LOVE

TROMBONE

Words and Music by JOHN LENNON
and PAUL McCARTNEY

Moderately

AND I LOVE HER

TROMBONE

Words and Music by JOHN LENNON
and PAUL McCARTNEY

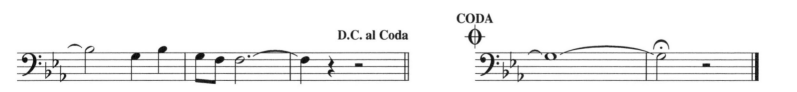

BACK IN THE U.S.S.R.

TROMBONE

Words and Music by JOHN LENNON
and PAUL McCARTNEY

THE BALLAD OF JOHN AND YOKO

TROMBONE

Words and Music by JOHN LENNON
and PAUL McCARTNEY

Moderate Rock

BECAUSE

TROMBONE

Words and Music by JOHN LENNON
and PAUL McCARTNEY

BIRTHDAY

TROMBONE

Words and Music by JOHN LENNON
and PAUL McCARTNEY

Moderately fast Rock

BLACKBIRD

TROMBONE

Words and Music by JOHN LENNON
and PAUL McCARTNEY

CAN'T BUY ME LOVE

TROMBONE

Words and Music by JOHN LENNON
and PAUL McCARTNEY

COME TOGETHER

TROMBONE

Words and Music by JOHN LENNON
and PAUL McCARTNEY

A Day in the Life

TROMBONE

Words and Music by JOHN LENNON
and PAUL McCARTNEY

DAY TRIPPER

TROMBONE

Words and Music by JOHN LENNON
and PAUL McCARTNEY

DEAR PRUDENCE

TROMBONE

Words and Music by JOHN LENNON
and PAUL McCARTNEY

DO YOU WANT TO KNOW A SECRET?

TROMBONE

Words and Music by JOHN LENNON
and PAUL McCARTNEY

DRIVE MY CAR

TROMBONE

Words and Music by JOHN LENNON
and PAUL McCARTNEY

Moderately, with a beat

EIGHT DAYS A WEEK

TROMBONE

Words and Music by JOHN LENNON
and PAUL McCARTNEY

ELEANOR RIGBY

TROMBONE

Words and Music by JOHN LENNON
and PAUL McCARTNEY

EVERY LITTLE THING

TROMBONE

Words and Music by JOHN LENNON
and PAUL McCARTNEY

THE FOOL ON THE HILL

TROMBONE

Words and Music by JOHN LENNON
and PAUL McCARTNEY

FROM ME TO YOU

TROMBONE

Words and Music by JOHN LENNON
and PAUL McCARTNEY

GET BACK

TROMBONE

*Words and Music by JOHN LENNON
and PAUL McCARTNEY*

GIRL

TROMBONE

Words and Music by JOHN LENNON
and PAUL McCARTNEY

GOLDEN SLUMBERS

TROMBONE

Words and Music by JOHN LENNON
and PAUL McCARTNEY

GOOD DAY SUNSHINE

TROMBONE

Words and Music by JOHN LENNON
and PAUL McCARTNEY

GOT TO GET YOU INTO MY LIFE

TROMBONE

Words and Music by JOHN LENNON
and PAUL McCARTNEY

A HARD DAY'S NIGHT

TROMBONE

Words and Music by JOHN LENNON
and PAUL McCARTNEY

HELLO, GOODBYE

TROMBONE

Words and Music by JOHN LENNON
and PAUL McCARTNEY

HELP!

TROMBONE

Words and Music by JOHN LENNON
and PAUL McCARTNEY

HELTER SKELTER

TROMBONE

Words and Music by JOHN LENNON
and PAUL McCARTNEY

HERE COMES THE SUN

TROMBONE

Words and Music by
GEORGE HARRISON

HERE, THERE AND EVERYWHERE

TROMBONE

Words and Music by JOHN LENNON
and PAUL McCARTNEY

HEY JUDE

TROMBONE

Words and Music by JOHN LENNON
and PAUL McCARTNEY

I FEEL FINE

TROMBONE

Words and Music by JOHN LENNON
and PAUL McCARTNEY

I AM THE WALRUS

TROMBONE

Words and Music by JOHN LENNON
and PAUL McCARTNEY

I SAW HER STANDING THERE

TROMBONE

Words and Music by JOHN LENNON
and PAUL McCARTNEY

Moderately bright, with a beat

I SHOULD HAVE KNOWN BETTER

TROMBONE

Words and Music by JOHN LENNON
and PAUL McCARTNEY

I WANT TO HOLD YOUR HAND

TROMBONE

Words and Music by JOHN LENNON
and PAUL McCARTNEY

I WILL

TROMBONE

Words and Music by JOHN LENNON
and PAUL McCARTNEY

I'LL CRY INSTEAD

TROMBONE

Words and Music by JOHN LENNON
and PAUL McCARTNEY

I'LL FOLLOW THE SUN

TROMBONE

Words and Music by JOHN LENNON
and PAUL McCARTNEY

I'M A LOSER

TROMBONE

Words and Music by JOHN LENNON
and PAUL McCARTNEY

I'M HAPPY JUST TO DANCE WITH YOU

TROMBONE

Words and Music by JOHN LENNON
and PAUL McCARTNEY

I'VE JUST SEEN A FACE

TROMBONE

Words and Music by JOHN LENNON
and PAUL McCARTNEY

IF I FELL

TROMBONE

Words and Music by JOHN LENNON
and PAUL McCARTNEY

IN MY LIFE

TROMBONE

Words and Music by JOHN LENNON
and PAUL McCARTNEY

IT WON'T BE LONG

TROMBONE

Words and Music by JOHN LENNON
and PAUL McCARTNEY

IT'S ONLY LOVE

TROMBONE

Words and Music by JOHN LENNON
and PAUL McCARTNEY

Moderately

JULIA

TROMBONE

Words and Music by JOHN LENNON
and PAUL McCARTNEY

LADY MADONNA

TROMBONE

Words and Music by JOHN LENNON
and PAUL McCARTNEY

LET IT BE

TROMBONE

Words and Music by JOHN LENNON
and PAUL McCARTNEY

THE LONG AND WINDING ROAD

TROMBONE

Words and Music by JOHN LENNON
and PAUL McCARTNEY

LOVE ME DO

TROMBONE

Words and Music by JOHN LENNON
and PAUL McCARTNEY

LUCY IN THE SKY WITH DIAMONDS

TROMBONE

Words and Music by JOHN LENNON
and PAUL McCARTNEY

MAGICAL MYSTERY TOUR

TROMBONE

Words and Music by JOHN LENNON
and PAUL McCARTNEY

MARTHA MY DEAR

TROMBONE

Words and Music by JOHN LENNON
and PAUL McCARTNEY

MICHELLE

TROMBONE

Words and Music by JOHN LENNON
and PAUL McCARTNEY

NO REPLY

TROMBONE

Words and Music by JOHN LENNON
and PAUL McCARTNEY

NORWEGIAN WOOD
(This Bird Has Flown)

TROMBONE

Words and Music by JOHN LENNON
and PAUL McCARTNEY

NOWHERE MAN

TROMBONE

Words and Music by JOHN LENNON
and PAUL McCARTNEY

OB-LA-DI, OB-LA-DA

TROMBONE

Words and Music by JOHN LENNON
and PAUL McCARTNEY

OCTOPUS'S GARDEN

TROMBONE

Words and Music by RICHARD STARKEY,
JOHN LENNON and PAUL McCARTNEY

PAPERBACK WRITER

TROMBONE

Words and Music by JOHN LENNON
and PAUL McCARTNEY

PENNY LANE

TROMBONE

Words and Music by JOHN LENNON
and PAUL McCARTNEY

PLEASE PLEASE ME

TROMBONE

Words and Music by JOHN LENNON
and PAUL McCARTNEY

P.S. I LOVE YOU

TROMBONE

Words and Music by JOHN LENNON
and PAUL McCARTNEY

REVOLUTION

TROMBONE

Words and Music by JOHN LENNON
and PAUL McCARTNEY

Moderate Rock and Roll Shuffle

RUN FOR YOUR LIFE

TROMBONE

Words and Music by JOHN LENNON
and PAUL McCARTNEY

SGT. PEPPER'S LONELY HEARTS CLUB BAND

TROMBONE

Words and Music by JOHN LENNON
and PAUL McCARTNEY

SHE LOVES YOU

TROMBONE

Words and Music by JOHN LENNON
and PAUL McCARTNEY

SHE'S A WOMAN

TROMBONE

Words and Music by JOHN LENNON
and PAUL McCARTNEY

SOMETHING

TROMBONE

Words and Music by
GEORGE HARRISON

STRAWBERRY FIELDS FOREVER

TROMBONE

Words and Music by JOHN LENNON
and PAUL McCARTNEY

TELL ME WHY

TROMBONE

Words and Music by JOHN LENNON
and PAUL McCARTNEY

THANK YOU GIRL

TROMBONE

Words and Music by JOHN LENNON
and PAUL McCARTNEY

THINGS WE SAID TODAY

TROMBONE

Words and Music by JOHN LENNON
and PAUL McCARTNEY

THIS BOY
(Ringo's Theme)

TROMBONE

Words and Music by JOHN LENNON
and PAUL McCARTNEY

Slow Rock & Roll

TICKET TO RIDE

TROMBONE

Words and Music by JOHN LENNON
and PAUL McCARTNEY

Moderate Rock

TWIST AND SHOUT

TROMBONE

Words and Music by BERT RUSSELL
and PHIL MEDLEY

WE CAN WORK IT OUT

TROMBONE

Words and Music by JOHN LENNON
and PAUL McCARTNEY

WHEN I'M SIXTY-FOUR

TROMBONE

Words and Music by JOHN LENNON
and PAUL McCARTNEY

WHILE MY GUITAR GENTLY WEEPS

TROMBONE

Words and Music by
GEORGE HARRISON

WITH A LITTLE HELP FROM MY FRIENDS

TROMBONE

Words and Music by JOHN LENNON
and PAUL McCARTNEY

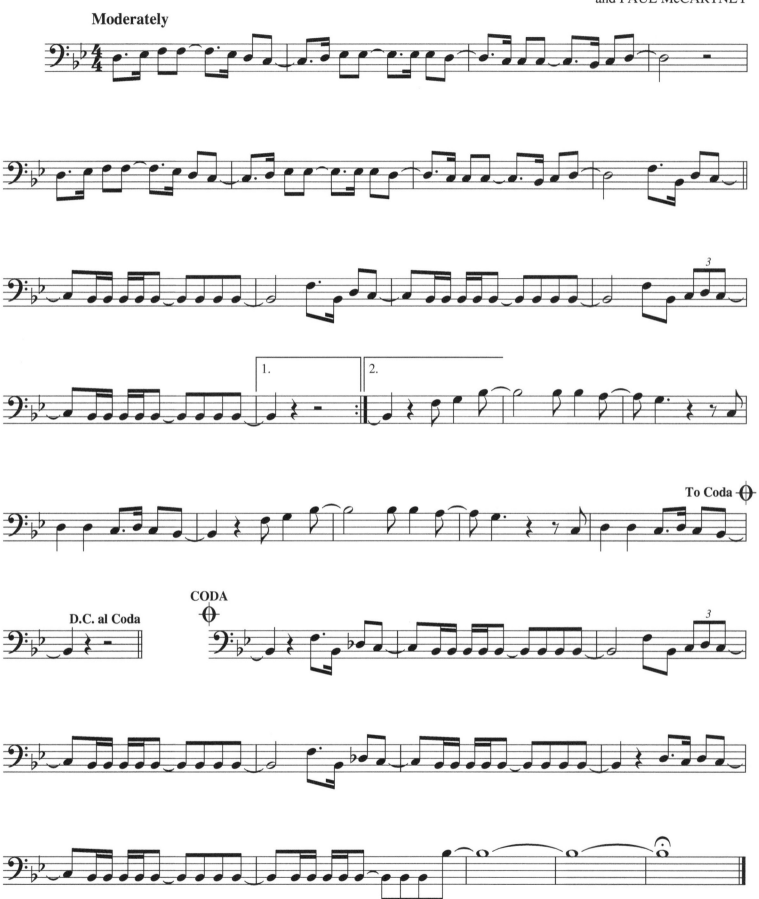

THE WORD

TROMBONE

Words and Music by JOHN LENNON
and PAUL McCARTNEY

YELLOW SUBMARINE

TROMBONE

Words and Music by JOHN LENNON
and PAUL McCARTNEY

YES IT IS

TROMBONE

Words and Music by JOHN LENNON
and PAUL McCARTNEY

YESTERDAY

TROMBONE

Words and Music by JOHN LENNON
and PAUL McCARTNEY

YOU CAN'T DO THAT

TROMBONE

Words and Music by JOHN LENNON
and PAUL McCARTNEY

YOU WON'T SEE ME

TROMBONE

Words and Music by JOHN LENNON
and PAUL McCARTNEY

YOU'RE GOING TO LOSE THAT GIRL

TROMBONE

Words and Music by JOHN LENNON
and PAUL McCARTNEY

YOU'VE GOT TO HIDE YOUR LOVE AWAY

TROMBONE

Words and Music by JOHN LENNON
and PAUL McCARTNEY

YOUR MOTHER SHOULD KNOW

TROMBONE

Words and Music by JOHN LENNON
and PAUL McCARTNEY